TABLE of CONTENTS

OPENING the WEST

In 1803 President Thomas Jefferson bought a huge piece of land stretching west from the Mississippi River to the Rocky Mountains and north from the Gulf of Mexico to the Canadian border. Called the Louisiana Purchase, it doubled the size of the United States. In 1804 Jefferson hired Meriwether Lewis and William Clark to explore this unknown land. With their Native American guide Sacagawea, Lewis and Clark explored the West from 1804 to 1806. They created maps, charted rivers, identified plants and animals, and brought back tales of harsh weather and beautiful land.

Mountain men, like Jim Bridger and James Beckwourth, followed Lewis and Clark. They blazed new trails, trapped beavers for fur, and led **expeditions** into the West. Soon, tales of the rich farmland, fine climate, and plentiful game convinced many people to move west. In 1848 gold was found in California. The movement west became a mad rush. Large numbers of people left home in search of free or cheap farmland, religious freedom, or gold. These people called themselves **emigrants** because they were leaving the United States and moving to lands that were then **territories.**

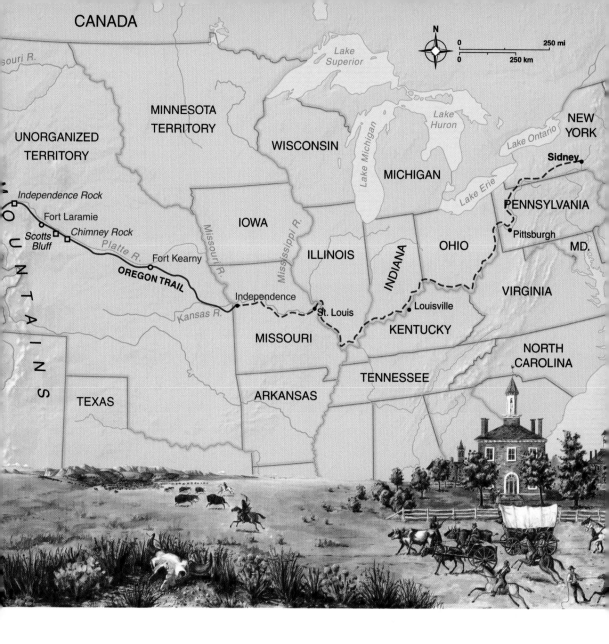

Between 1840 and 1860 somewhere between 300,000 and 500,000 emigrants traveled westward on the Oregon Trail.

MEET THE MARSHALL FAMILY

In 1852 the Marshall family from Sidney, New York, decided to move west. They planned to join relatives already settled in the Oregon Territory. Their diaries and letters tell of life on their journey west.

William Marshall, father

Harriet Marshall, mother

Tom Marshall, 16

Henry Marshall, 6

Sarah Marshall, 12

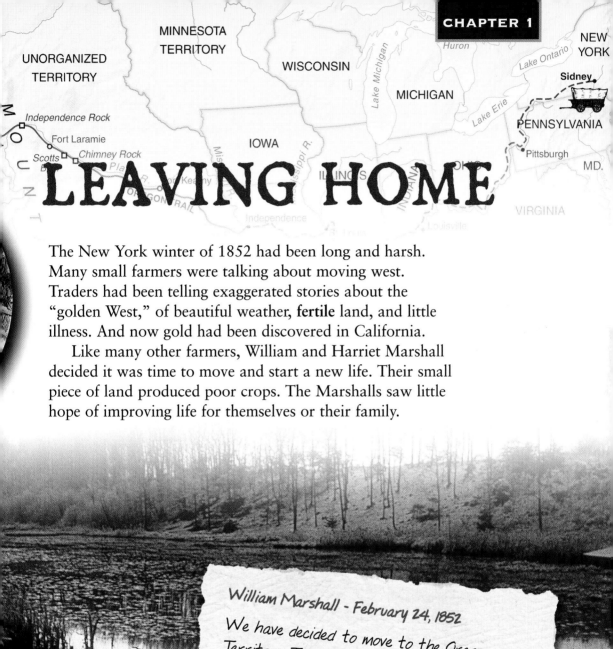

CHAPTER 1

LEAVING HOME

The New York winter of 1852 had been long and harsh. Many small farmers were talking about moving west. Traders had been telling exaggerated stories about the "golden West," of beautiful weather, **fertile** land, and little illness. And now gold had been discovered in California.

Like many other farmers, William and Harriet Marshall decided it was time to move and start a new life. Their small piece of land produced poor crops. The Marshalls saw little hope of improving life for themselves or their family.

William Marshall - February 24, 1852

We have decided to move to the Oregon Territory. The land is free and the soil is rich. Harriet wants to go, too, but she will miss her friends. She will make new ones. Tom and Henry are excited. Poor Sarah does not want to go.

They decided to join Harriet's sister Liddy and her husband, James Thomas, in the Oregon Territory. Once there, William and Harriet could get 320 acres of farmland by living on the land and improving it over four years. With that much land, they believed they and their children could live a better life. The Marshalls had to raise about $800 to pay for their trip.

Sarah Marshall - February 26, 1852

The neighbors gave us a farewell party. They are all sad to see us go. Mrs. Smith gave Mama some lovely lace handkerchiefs and a calico shirt for Papa. Mrs. Ketchum gave us bonnets and hats for the boys because she heard the sun is harsh in the West. Others gave us aprons, blankets, quilts, jams, mustard, pickles, lots of dried fruit and beans, and bread. Mr. Black gave us new shoes. He said we'd need them walking to Oregon. It is about 2,000 miles. Papa got a new rifle. Tom will get Papa's old one. Henry wants a gun, too, but Mama says he is too young. I have to learn to drive the wagon and herd the sheep. So does Tom. I hope I can do it.

Tomorrow I say good-bye to my best friend, Emily. She gave me a birthday card because I will be gone on my birthday. I miss her already. She took home my cat, Smoky. I made a beautiful basket for him to sleep in. Emily said Smoky will sleep in her room. It will take us almost six months to get to Oregon. I am scared. Tom claims he is excited, but I think he is scared, too. I know Mama is. What will happen to us?

Harriet Marshall - February 26, 1852

I finally heard from my sister Liddy. She says Oregon is beautiful. They built a log cabin by a river. She has planted flowers. Liddy loves flowers. Hopefully we will see them next fall. We leave for Independence tomorrow. We sold my organ to the music teacher and his family. It is too large to take with us. Last night I played all our favorite songs. I will miss my friend, the organ. But we will sing on the Trail.

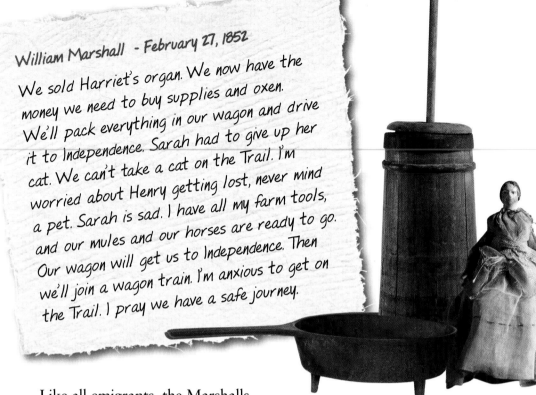

William Marshall - February 27, 1852

We sold Harriet's organ. We now have the money we need to buy supplies and oxen. We'll pack everything in our wagon and drive it to Independence. Sarah had to give up her cat. We can't take a cat on the Trail. I'm worried about Henry getting lost, never mind a pet. Sarah is sad. I have all my farm tools, and our mules and our horses are ready to go. Our wagon will get us to Independence. Then we'll join a wagon train. I'm anxious to get on the Trail. I pray we have a safe journey.

Like all emigrants, the Marshalls had to decide what to pack for the long journey to the Oregon Territory. The wagons had little room for things that could not be used on the Trail.

Some of the items emigrants took with them were pans, a butter churner, and a doll.

Most emigrants packed dishes, pots and pans, tools, clothes, firearms, and bedding. They often packed a few favorite pieces of family furniture, too. Sometimes they had to abandon them along the Trail to lighten their wagons to make it up the steep mountains.

The Marshalls first traveled from upstate New York to Pittsburgh, Pennsylvania, next to Louisville, Kentucky, then to St. Louis, Missouri, and finally to Independence, Missouri. Independence was a "jumping-off" point for traveling along the Oregon Trail. Here the emigrants could buy supplies, join a wagon train, and wait for spring to begin their trip. By beginning their journey in mid-April, the emigrants could reach the Oregon Territory before the winter snows.

CHAPTER 2

WAITING for SPRING

By early spring the **prairie** outside Independence was full of emigrants. They were waiting to set out on the Trail. When the spring grass along the Trail was high enough to feed the livestock, the wagons would leave. The animals had to live off the land as the many wagon trains moved westward. But the emigrants couldn't wait too long to set off because of the threat of early snow in the mountains by September. As a result, everyone traveled along the Trail at once.

William Marshall - April 2, 1852

My brother-in-law, James, wrote me. He says to leave Missouri with a good light wagon, 150 lbs. of flour, 60 lbs. of bacon, 40 lbs. of sugar, 25 lbs. of dried fruit, 10 lbs. of rice, plenty of pickles, vinegar, coffee and tea, and lots of warm blankets. I had a wagon built with a toolbox, a place for a water barrel, and hardwood brakes. The brakes might save our lives. He said to buy a spare axle, too. There will be little room in the wagon—four feet by ten feet. Tom and I will have to walk or ride. I'll teach Sarah how to drive the wagon. She'll have to walk too, herding the sheep. Tomorrow I sign us up for a wagon train. We hope to leave in two weeks. The talk about crossing the rivers makes me jumpy. I'll try to save some money to take ferries.

Harriet Marshall - April 3, 1852

Our wagon is called a prairie schooner. It looks like a ship at sea. It has red wheels, a blue body, and a bright, white canvas top. There are two tops, and they are coated with linseed oil to protect us from the rain. It is pretty but it is not home. We have been camping in the wagon. Luckily the weather is warm. Cooking outside is hard. The wind blows out the fire before I can get it started. Sarah is lonely. She hates herding. Tom thinks he's all grown up and a man. Henry does, too. I fear for them. Pride leads to mistakes. I so miss my organ and my friends singing around it. A woman here has a piano and she lets me play it. She is taking it with her. William says it won't reach Oregon. We bought lots of quinine, hartshorn for snake bites, and castor oil. I hope these medicines will protect us on the Trail.

The emigrants began final preparations. Independence became a hub of activity. People, animals, and wagons filled the streets. Blacksmiths hammered constantly in their sheds, building and repairing wagons and shoeing horses, mules, and oxen. Shops bustled as emigrants scrambled to buy supplies before shortages drove up prices or food ran out. A family of four needed over a thousand pounds of food for the 2,000-mile journey.

Upon arriving in Independence, the Marshalls set up camp and began to prepare for their long journey west.

April 7, 1852
Independence, Missouri

Dear Emily,

There are all kinds of people here, most of them nice. The camp is like a small town. The girl camped next to us likes Tom. He says no, but she does. Mama just laughs. Papa tries not to laugh at him. Tom sort of struts by the girl's wagon.

There is so much to do. Mama and I have to dry food, store it, and wash all the clothes. My fingers are red from washing things in the river. And I miss my bed. My bedding is hard and cold. Everyone says this is nothing compared to life on the Trail. I'm glad I have my diary. Papa says I can ride Henry's horse for some of the journey. Henry says no, but I will. Some rich people are going out west, too. They have a wagon just for their servants. The women wear these strange pants-like things called bloomers. Mama says I will wear dresses. We'll see. I don't want to walk over 2,000 miles in a dress.

Today I tried to cook over an open fire. I nearly burnt my hand. I guess we'll eat a lot of stew on the Trail because it's easy to cook over a fire. No more roast pig or venison for me. Papa says to enjoy the meat now. I hope we have meat on the journey. I hate beans. How's Smoky? Write to me. Miss you.

Your best friend,
Sarah Marshall

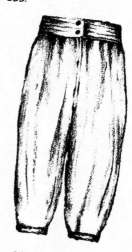

Bloomers

Spring finally arrived. The emigrants were anxious to begin their journey. They joined different wagon trains, choosing carefully to find a train with a good wagon master.

The wagon master and the pilot, or scout, were critical to the success of the wagon train. They mapped out the journey and made decisions about which routes to take. The wagon masters were often former mountain men who knew both the Native Americans and the region well. The pilot would travel ahead of the wagons to deal with any problems along the Trail, such as fallen trees, or rocks, or hills too steep for the wagons. Often, the pilot or the wagon master spoke at least one Native American language.

The Marshalls joined a wagon train leaving on April 17, the day before Sarah's birthday. They thought it was a good sign. Their wagon master said he had traveled with the famous mountain men, Jim Bridger and Jedediah Smith. The Marshalls began their journey westward. Their goal was to reach Fort Kearny, Nebraska, by May. At this military post built to protect the emigrants along the Trail, they could buy fresh supplies.

CHAPTER 3

STARTING OUT

As dawn broke, the emigrants began to stir. The wagon master gave the signal and a bugle played. Nearly one hundred wagons started to move. Close to 400 people were leaving for the Oregon Trail this morning. The wagons looked like waves moving across the prairie. The Marshalls' wagon joined the others. On their first day along the Trail they walked almost fifteen miles.

That night they camped at the Shawnee Mission in Kansas where some of the emigrants saw their first Native Americans. Shawnee children were taught English and agriculture at the Mission. The Marshalls slept outside their wagon on the hard ground. Exhausted, they quickly fell asleep.

Sarah Marshall - April 19, 1852

I walked fifteen miles today in the blazing sun. My feet are covered with blisters. Mama said I should try walking barefoot. Boots are useless. The dust was so thick that Tom wrote words on Henry's forehead with spit. Henry'll know a lot of new words by Oregon. A lady in the wagon in front of us counts the graves. Henry helps her. In two days they have counted twelve. I herd the animals and ignore the graves. The sheep keep wandering off, and I have to get them. By the end of the day I long for sleep but am too tired to sleep. All around us are sheep, cattle, horses, people, and DUST. How I miss my room at home. There is nowhere to be alone.

15

William Marshall - April 26, 1852

We took a ferry across the Kansas River. It's safer than trying to float the wagon across. All of us thought the ferry might tip over from the weight, but we made it. The rivers are dangerous. You can't see the rocks. Animals get scared and pull people under the water. I will try to save money for more ferries. I'm hiding the money in my hat.

Harriet Marshall - April 27, 1852

We are at Alcove Spring. It is beautiful. There's lots of clean water and trees here. We had a picnic under a tree at lunchtime. We will rest here for an extra day. Sarah soaked her blistered feet in the spring. I rinsed out clothes. William and the children swam. If only the rest of the Trail could be like this.

Sarah Marshall - April 29, 1852

I hated to leave Alcove Spring. Swimming was wonderful. We had to pay a toll to cross the river at Rock Creek Station—10 cents. The man said it looked like that was all we could afford. Pa just smiled and tipped his hat. We still have not seen any buffalo yet. But we find their chips. We use the buffalo chips for fuel, the harder and drier the better. Papa says we'll see some buffalo soon. I'd like to see one.

William Marshall - May 3, 1852

We saw buffalo today, thousands of them as far as the eye could see. The wagon master stopped the train. A party of men went off to hunt the buffalo. Tom joined them. I told him to be careful to stay out of the line of fire! All morning we heard shots, but the men came back with only three buffalo. We all set about carving them up. I felt bad leaving the carcasses, but there's no time to dry the skin! We'll dry the meat and use it later in stews.

Sarah Marshall - May 4, 1852

A herd of buffalo stampeded by. It was a sight I will never forget. We had to wait for over two hours for all of them to pass! They are gigantic. I got out my pencils and sketched them. Tom bragged about how he helped shoot one of the buffalo. Henry wants to keep one for a pet. Mama laughed and said no. Henry wrote a note on one of the buffalo skulls to leave beside the Trail. Others had done the same.

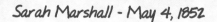

Harriet Marshall - May 5, 1852

I cooked buffalo meat for the first time last night. It is like deer meat but tastes gamier. But what a welcome change after days of bacon and bread. We saw many dead buffalo along the Trail. They are magnificent creatures. I feel sorry that we must kill them.

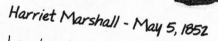

William Marshall - May 7, 1852

We have reached Fort Kearny. It is just a bunch of sod buildings, not a big fort. I'm not sure how it would protect us. But we can buy food here. Also, we all got letters. Harriet got some letters from her sister, and I heard from James. The worst is yet to come, according to his letters. We will rest here for three days. Poor Sarah's feet need it. Tom is supposed to be helping her with chores, but he seems distracted by a girl in the wagon behind us.

Fort Kearny was the first military post built to protect the Oregon Trail emigrants. But it wasn't the sturdy, walled town they expected. Still, the fort was an important stopping point where emigrants could buy fresh food and other supplies. It was also a place where some of the emigrants, already discouraged, decided to turn back.

At this point many emigrants began to lighten their wagon loads. Crossing rivers with heavy wagons was dangerous. If the wagons tipped over, all was lost. The Trail became littered with furniture, food, and other belongings that were not essential for the trip. **Scavengers** came out from Independence to collect the things the emigrants left on the Trail. They either kept them or sold them to new emigrants arriving in Independence.

Determined to reach the Oregon Territory, the Marshalls pushed ahead. Thoughts of uniting with Harriet's family and beginning a new life on their own large and fertile farm drove them onward.

CHAPTER 4

ALONG the TRAIL

The emigrants came to understand the harsh realities of their journey as they passed by the many graves along the Trail. Many of the emigrants died during **cholera epidemics**. Cholera was caused by bacteria, which thrived in the crowded, unsanitary campgrounds along the Trail. The emigrants could do little to prevent or cure cholera. Cholera resulted in severe diarrhea, heavy sweating, and often vomiting. The sick died very quickly.

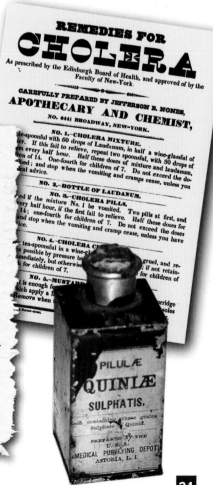

Harriet Marshall - May 13, 1852

All it seems to do is rain. Everything is soaked. Nothing ever dries. Many families have sick ones. We leave them behind and hope they find us. Medicine does not seem to help. But I make William, Tom, Sarah, and Henry take castor oil every day. I had to chase Henry to make him take it. William says we will soon be at Courthouse Rock. We found the grave of my nephew, Liddy's son. We prayed over it and left flowers. I fear losing a child on this journey.

Other emigrants died from accidents. Inexperienced around animals and wagons, some were trampled or killed by falls. Others drowned during river crossings. Families stood on the banks watching helplessly as their loved ones were swept away. Still others were killed during fierce lightning storms. The graves along the Trail were a constant reminder of how dangerous the journey was.

Sarah Marshall - May 17, 1852

I walked ten miles today. We left behind two wagons. The people were very sick. I'm glad we saw Courthouse Rock. It is beautiful and looks just like a castle. We carved our names at the top. All we see now are dead oxen or graves. There are lots of bones shining in the hot sun. Henry and Mrs. Harris have counted 98 graves. She wears black and just sits there counting. Tom calls her Grim Reaper. I'm going to mail my drawing of Courthouse Rock to Emily.

Harriet Marshall - May 22, 1852

Henry's friend died today. He was well, he got sick, and then he died, all in three hours. Poor Henry went from counting graves to digging them. I worry so about our family.

William Marshall - June 3, 1852

At last we are at Chimney Rock. Chimney Rock is better than Courthouse Rock! It's like a huge spiral going up into the sky. Henry and Tom tried to climb it but couldn't. I felt like a bug standing next to it. It's almost four hundred feet high. We'll rest here for a few days. Then it's on to Fort Laramie. We'll all be happy to see some civilization.

Sarah Marshall - June 4, 1852

I'm glad to rest here at Chimney Rock. It is so tall, and it looks like a giant pen. I drew a picture of it. I'll send it to Emily when we get to Fort Laramie. I hope there are some letters there for me. I am tired of just talking to the sheep during the day. Elizabeth, the girl who herds the animals with me, only seems to want to talk to Tom.

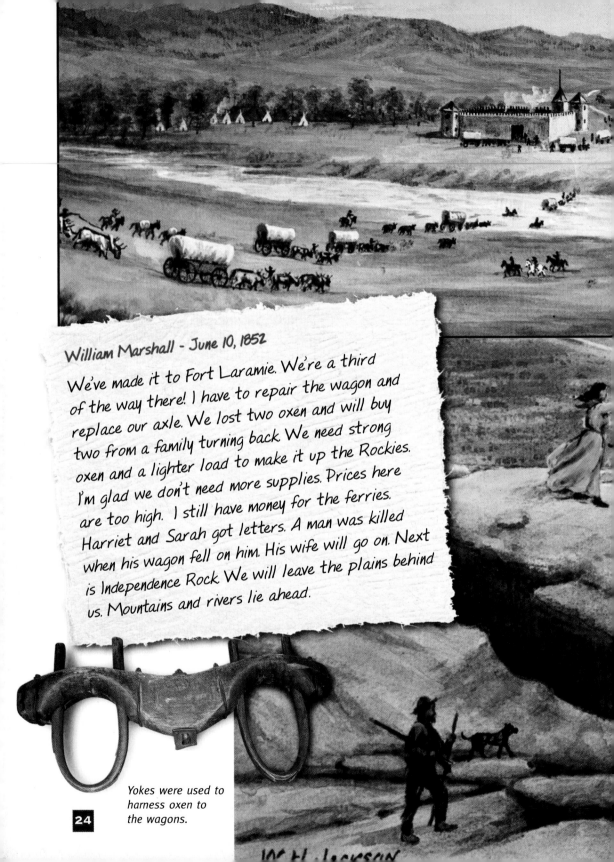

William Marshall - June 10, 1852

We've made it to Fort Laramie. We're a third of the way there! I have to repair the wagon and replace our axle. We lost two oxen and will buy two from a family turning back. We need strong oxen and a lighter load to make it up the Rockies. I'm glad we don't need more supplies. Prices here are too high. I still have money for the ferries. Harriet and Sarah got letters. A man was killed when his wagon fell on him. His wife will go on. Next is Independence Rock. We will leave the plains behind us. Mountains and rivers lie ahead.

Yokes were used to harness oxen to the wagons.

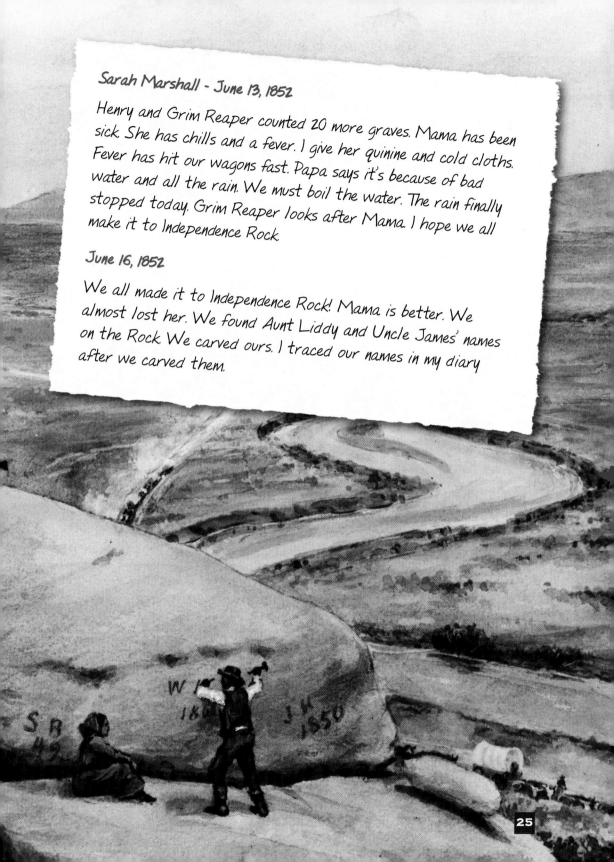

Sarah Marshall - June 13, 1852

Henry and Grim Reaper counted 20 more graves. Mama has been sick. She has chills and a fever. I give her quinine and cold cloths. Fever has hit our wagons fast. Papa says it's because of bad water and all the rain. We must boil the water. The rain finally stopped today. Grim Reaper looks after Mama. I hope we all make it to Independence Rock.

June 16, 1852

We all made it to Independence Rock! Mama is better. We almost lost her. We found Aunt Liddy and Uncle James' names on the Rock. We carved ours. I traced our names in my diary after we carved them.

South Pass was one of the most important **landmarks** on the Oregon Trail. A valley twenty miles wide, South Pass allowed the emigrants to travel through the mountains rather than climb over them. South Pass also was the fork in the Trail where the emigrants decided whether to head northwest to the Oregon Territory or southwest to California.

The emigrants had to get through the mountains before it snowed. At South Pass they heard the story of the Donner party. In 1846 this group of settlers was traveling west when they became stranded by early snows in the Sierra Nevada Mountains. Most of the party died. No emigrant wanted to suffer that fate. Everyone was anxious to continue the journey and stay ahead of the snows.

CHAPTER 5

MAKING FRIENDS

The emigrants heard many frightening tales about the Native American nations, such as the Pawnee, Sioux, Shoshone, and Bannock who lived along the Oregon Trail. Many of these tales were false. Wagon trains were not regularly attacked by the Native Americans.

Native American trails formed the paths that the emigrants followed on their journey westward. Some Native Americans worked as guides, using their skills and canoes to help emigrants safely cross the rivers and mountains.

William Marshall - July 18, 1852

Last night a few Nez Percé came to our camp. They were friendly. Some in our party reached for their rifles, but the wagon master kept the peace. The Nez Percé looked at our horses. They had an extra horse with them. I traded coffee, a silver belt buckle, and tobacco for the horse. It will replace Henry's horse that died. Henry claims the horse's name is Running Wind. Just hope the horse makes it to Oregon. Snake River is next.

By the time the emigrants reached Fort Hall on the Snake River, many were running low on supplies, and their animals were dead or dying. Once the emigrants realized the Native Americans were not going to attack their wagon train, they bartered with them. They exchanged clothing and tools for fresh food, herbs, moccasins, and other useful goods.

The Marshalls were able to barter for much needed items with the Nez Percé. The Nez Percé also helped them to cross a difficult and frightening part of the Trail.

Harriet Marshall - July 25, 1852

Today, the Nez Percé helped us cross a narrow part of the Snake River. This was our first time in a canoe. Sarah was scared, but I felt safe. We paid $2 to the Nez Percé to guide our horses and cattle across the river. They swam beside the animals. We lost one cow in the crossing, but all the other animals made it safely. Sarah was hoping some sheep would be lost. There are three islands in the river. The Indians showed us how to use them as stepping stones. Some in our party who crossed on their own lost wagons, animals, or even loved ones.

Sarah Marshall - July 26, 1852

The canoe ride was scary, but we didn't tip over. Some wagons did tip over and were lost. Two boys were lost, also. Water just swirled up and got them. We couldn't do anything. I'm glad we had the Nez Percé to help us. The banks of the river were covered with dead cattle that had washed up. Henry is riding his new horse. He says the horse rides like the wind.

August 13

I walked ten miles in the rain. Mama tried to stay dry, but the canvas leaks. Henry rode his horse wearing Papa's huge coat. It kept him dry but he sure looked funny. I hope Mama doesn't get sick. We spent the night drying things around the fire.

Native Americans helped many of the emigrants cross the Snake River. Although crossing the river was the fastest way to Fort Boise, it was also the most dangerous. The currents of the Snake River were strong, and many wagons and animals were lost. So many emigrants lost animals in the Snake River that it was called the "cattle graveyard."

The next stop on the Trail was Fort Boise. Fort Boise was plagued by floods. Three years after the Marshalls visited it, Fort Boise was gone. By this point on the Trail, supplies were low, and many animals were sick or weakened. Wagons were in poor condition. People were tired. Fall was approaching. Yet many challenges still lay ahead.

CHAPTER 6

FORDING the RIVER

The emigrants were now on the last leg of their long, hard journey. They had reached the end of the Trail, blocked by the Cascade Mountains. Here, at a place called The Dalles, emigrants had to pass down the wide Columbia River, full of **whirlpools** and **rapids.** Its banks were high and rocky. Few could afford the ferry that traveled down the river. Those without the fare had to float their wagons down the river.

Some emigrants chose to go through the Cascade Mountains on the Barlow Road. This route had steep, narrow paths covered with roots, rocks, and boulders. The emigrants used ropes and pulleys to pull their wagons up and over the mountains. Some wagons slipped out of the pulleys, crashing down hillsides and sometimes crushing emigrants.

The Marshalls had saved $16.00 to pay for the ferry. But they had to wait two weeks before they could get onto the ferry. There were too many people and not enough boats.

William Marshall - September 8, 1852

We sent out search parties for some people lost in the mountains. Hope they find them. We will wait for the ferry. Luckily we have the money. One family from our wagon train was lost when their wagon sank in the river. Relatives watched but could do nothing. Rocks seem to appear out of nowhere. We eat, sleep, sing songs, and wait. We can use the rest.

Sarah Marshall - September 11, 1852

Our campground is like a small village next to the river. We watch people trying to get across. Fights break out. I am just glad I don't have to walk. And there's no sheep to herd! We sold them. Poor things. Some were lost crossing the river. I feel bad.

Harriet Marshall - September 17

Yesterday two brothers fought over where to cross the river. They were so mad they cut their wagon in half. Both just took off with half a wagon. It was sad and funny. Tempers are short now that we are so close. I'm thankful for the rest. Sarah's feet are raw. Henry is forbidden to go near the river. I hope we can get on the ferry soon.

The Marshalls finally took the ferry down the Columbia River. During the trip, the oxen all shuffled to one side and nearly tipped the ferry. William struggled to keep the animals quiet and calm. Harriet held on to Henry to keep him from falling off the ferry. Sarah clutched her diary and crossed her fingers. But at last they landed. They had little money left, but they had arrived in Oregon Territory near the Willamette Valley.

The weather was rainy. But to the emigrants, the land looked lush and green. They gathered their belongings, hitched up their wagons, and set off on the last few miles to Oregon City. Once there, the emigrants would search for family and then settle down.

On the Trail the emigrants had an expression, "seeing the elephant," which meant that they had suffered hardships or misfortune. Reaching Oregon City meant that the emigrants had finally put the elephant behind them.

CHAPTER 7

REACHING OREGON CITY

The emigrants moved even faster now. They were desperate to reach Oregon City, claim land, and begin their new lives. Supplies were very low. Water was nearly gone. The emigrants boiled the river water. They did not want to become ill this close to their goal.

Upon reaching Oregon City, the wagon train broke up. Friends said good-bye. Their journey was over. They had made it. Oregon City looked like a wonderful city to the emigrants. It had buildings, stores, and inns. At last they could sleep in beds and not on the ground.

The Marshalls said good-bye to friends and decided to rest before setting out for the Thomas' home. Harriet and Sarah wanted a bath. Henry wanted an ice cream. William was just thankful they had all reached Oregon safely. The family looked for a letter from Tom, but there was none. But Sarah had a letter from Emily.

Oregon City

September 3, 1852
Sidney, New York

Dear Sarah,

I hope this letter finds you safe. What is Oregon City like? Is it like Albany? Is it a big city or is it tiny like our town? What will your new home be like?

Mama talks about my becoming a teacher. She says I am smart. What do you think? Maybe I could come out to the Oregon Territory and teach.

Life here is just the same. The minister still gives long sermons. Papa pretends to listen. Mama wears a new hat when she can. And of course, she carries her lace handkerchiefs.

There is a new boy in town. He is fourteen. His name is John. His family lives down the road. Mama says he is quite nice. I hope she doesn't have any ideas.

Write soon. I want to hear about your new home. I miss you!

STILL your best friend,
Emily Smith

October 12, 1852
Oregon City, Oregon

Dear Emily,

Thank you for writing me so many letters. At night, when it was cold and I was scared and lonely, I read your letters. They gave me something to look forward to. At long last, our trip is over!

Oregon City is like heaven compared to the Trail. There are churches, stores, blacksmith shops, and a newspaper. Papa bought a paper yesterday and read it aloud. Henry bought an ice cream, and I got some candy. Mama bought a small piece of silk. She is making your mama something. She traded a calico shirt your mama made for moccasins for me!

In a few days we go to Portland. I miss the friends I made on the Trail. You can't walk 2,000 miles and not make friends! But I miss you most of all. I hope you do become a teacher. Then you could come out here! It is beautiful, and the grass is so green.

I'll tell you all about our new home in my next letter!

Still your best friend,
Sarah

Oregon City, 1850s

The Marshalls signed up for their land. William and Harriet became successful farmers. They learned to love their new home. Harriet wrote and spoke about her experiences as a woman landowner.

Emily never came to Oregon. She married and stayed in the East. Sarah and Emily continued to write to each other. They remained best friends. Sarah became a teacher and later married.

Henry became a captain on a steamship. He loved the rivers but remembered their dangers. Tom never found gold, but he ran a successful hotel for people coming to California. He and Elizabeth married and had six children.

The Rocky Mountains

GLOSSARY

cholera - a disease of the stomach and intestines that causes cramps and vomiting and sometimes death

emigrant - a person who leaves his or her own country in order to live in another one

epidemic - the rapid spreading of a disease quickly through a community

expedition - a long journey for a special purpose, such as exploring

fertile - good for growing crops and plants

landmark - an object in a landscape that can be seen from far away

prairie - a large area of flat or rolling grassland with few or no trees

rapids - a place in a river where the water flows very fast

scavenger - someone or something that searches among garbage for food or useful things

territory - a part of the United States not admitted as a state

whirlpool - a current of water that moves quickly in a circle and pulls floating objects toward its center